Ham and Chicken Do Spain

By Kimberly Naylor

Illustrated by Lei Yang

Spain is in southwestern Europe
with Africa at its tip.
Because of its position,
it's been a part of many trips.

Migrants came from all over
looking for somewhere brand new.
Then the Romans came down
and said, "Hey, we think we'll stay too."

For the next 500 years,
Spain belonged to Rome.
And then something happened;
the Moors began to roam.

They were from North Africa.
They came up and invaded.
Taking over most of Spain,
a Muslim land was created.

Then on one fine day
in 1469,
a king asked a queen,
"Would you please be mine?"

Ferdinand wed Isabella
and their two kingdoms <u>merged</u>.
They became the <u>Catholic Monarchs</u>,
and their power <u>surged</u>.

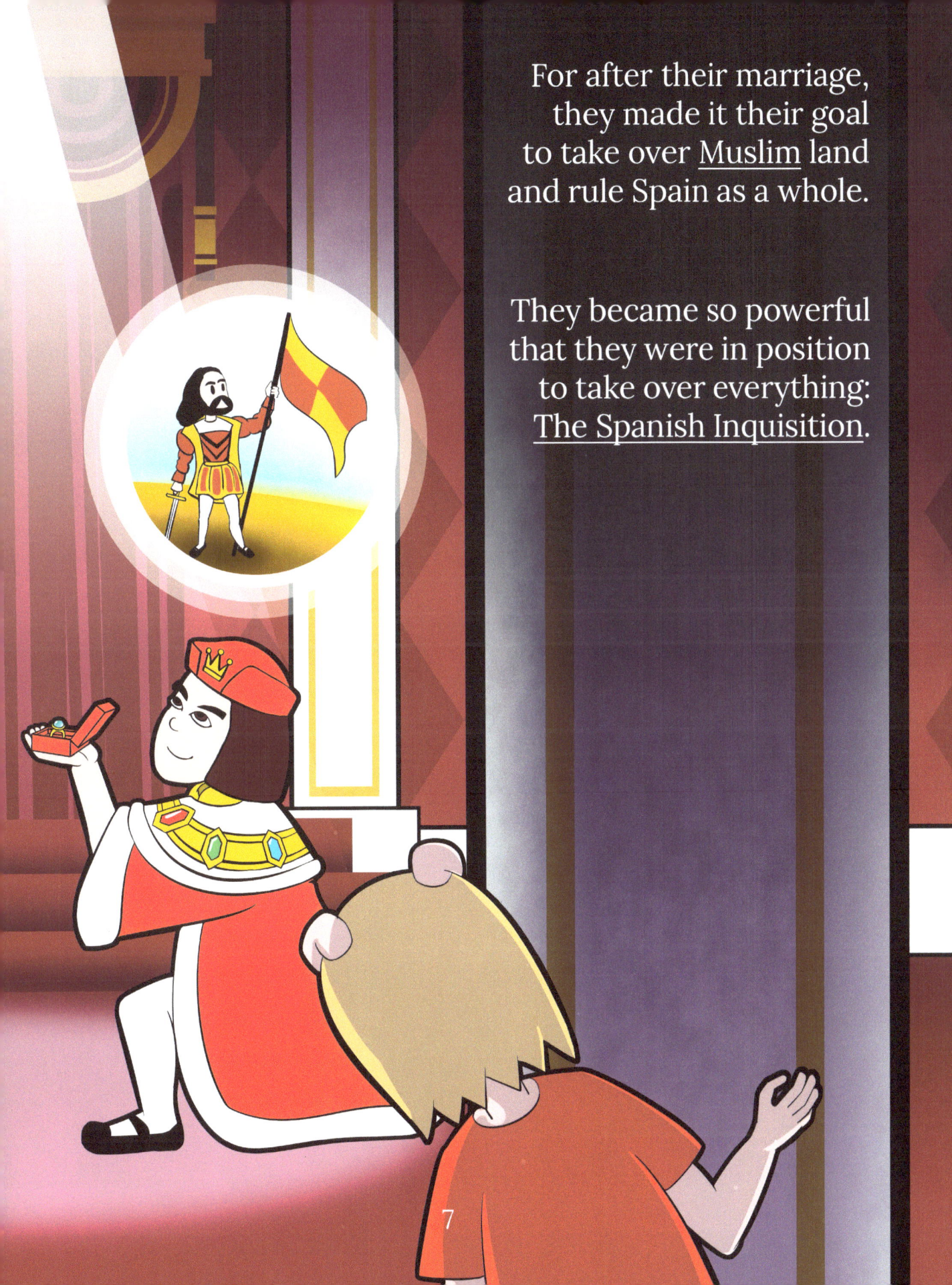

For after their marriage, they made it their goal to take over Muslim land and rule Spain as a whole.

They became so powerful that they were in position to take over everything: The Spanish Inquisition.

And sail he did
to the New World and more
bringing back exotic things
from many a far-off shore.

Santa Maria

Their explorations and conquests
proved the earth is round.
And because of their discoveries,
new trade routes were found.

It's also the reason
why Spanish is spoken all around.

Today Spain is modern
and has a <u>constitution</u>
but it still has a king;
it's kind of a <u>fusion</u>.

We'll start at the capital.
It sits in the middle like a heart.
Madrid beats with life and culture.
Naturally, it's where we'll start.

We'll meet you at the big square.
It's called the Plaza Mayor.
It's the perfect meeting place
to decide what to explore.

Here is the San Miguel Market.
It is right next-door.
We can try so many different dishes.
There is tapas galore!

Order one after another;
it's really a good deal.
Tapas is another word
for sampling many mini meals.

Let's head to Pamplona.
You are in for a treat!
To see the Running of the Bulls,
you must be quick on your feet.

Racing towards the bullfighting ring,
the energy rush is fun.
But to avoid the six bulls,
you must run, run, run, run, run!!

Now we're off to Barcelona.
It sits here on the east coast.
Back in 1992,
it was the Olympic host.

Have you ever been to the beach
and made a castle out of wet sand,
slowly letting it all
drip from your hand?

Church of the Sacred Family
looks like this a bit.
Even though it's not finished,
it's still a big hit!

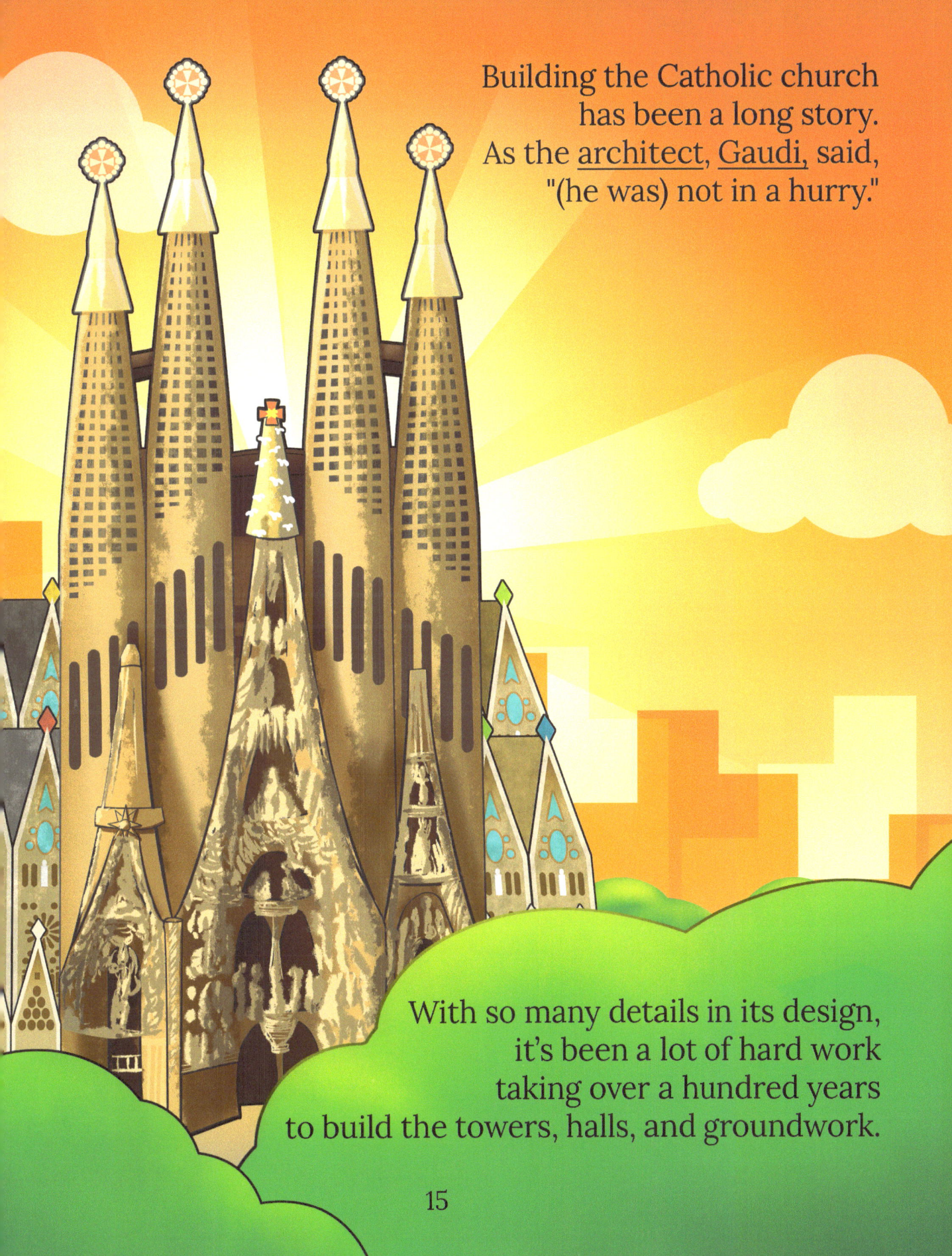

Building the Catholic church has been a long story. As the architect, Gaudi, said, "(he was) not in a hurry."

With so many details in its design, it's been a lot of hard work taking over a hundred years to build the towers, halls, and groundwork.

Park Guell is our next stop
up on the hill straight ahead.
The buildings are decorated
like houses made of gingerbread.

The mosaics are so colorful
and can be found all over the park.
Gaudi's architecture
make this place a true landmark.

The walls twist and turn like a snake
and have built-in seats
where we can take a nap, or "siesta" (see-es-tuh),
and a place to rest our feet.

Naps make me feel better
and now my energy is back.
It's time for La Tomatina,
the world's largest food fight!...

WHACK!!!

There are some rules to this fight:
Only tomatoes can be tossed.
It makes the streets look like
they've all been tomato sauced.

Now off to the Alhambra,
to the big "fortress of red."
It was also used as a home
for the <u>Muslim</u> rulers who led.

Once a sparkling white palace,
the sun turned it red.
The gardens here are lovely,
the grounds beautiful to <u>tread</u>.

It is in this area of Spain
or in the areas near,
where it is said the guitar
was created here.

They took the Arab lute
and then added a sixth string.
The sound that it made
has helped many a singer sing.

Let's head southwest
to the city of Seville,
a perfect place to ride bikes
because it's flat with no hills.

Let's go get a map
and hop on our bikes to search.
They say it's hard to miss
the world's largest gothic church.

All the way down south,
all the way at the tip,
lies The Strait of Gibraltar,
a thin watery strip.

At its narrowest point,
it's almost eight miles wide.
If you stand on the edge of Spain,
you'll see <u>Africa</u> on the other side.

Do you recognize this painting?
It was important to learn, we felt,
that it was done by <u>Salvador Dali</u>.
I wonder what made that clock melt.

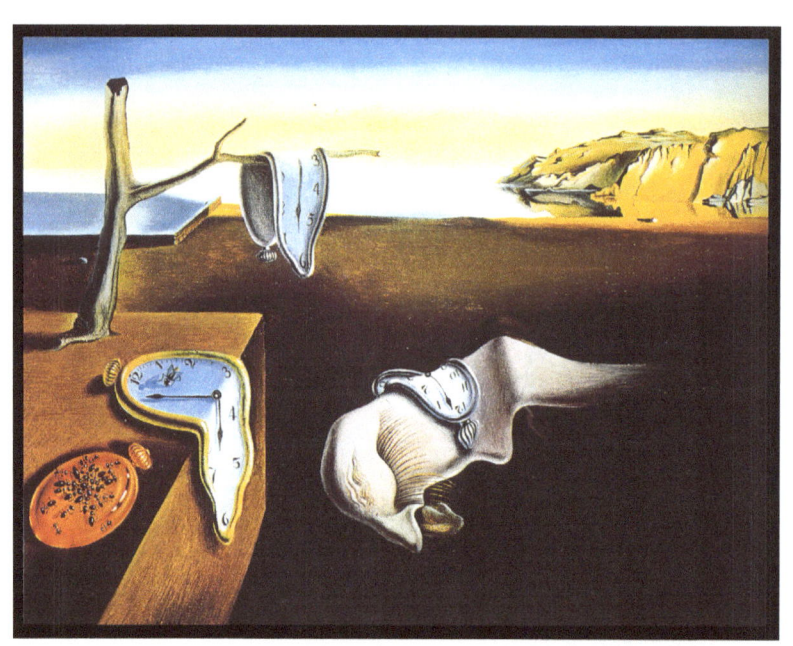

The Persistence of Memory

Guernica

Here are some more paintings.
Pablo Picasso painted these.
What's happening in Guernica?
And what do you think that girl sees?

Girl Before A Mirror

Why is the old guitarist so sad?
Maybe he was kicked out of his band.
It's interesting to look at these paintings
and try to fully understand.

The Old Guitarist

Before our trip is over,
before it is said and done,
you'll want to learn to dance <u>flamenco</u>.
They say it's really fun!

Boys, bring your dancing shoes;
girls, your long red dress.
Chicken will show you how.
We know you will impress.

Shake your hips,
hands go clap clap,
step this way,
fingers go snap snap.

Now it's time to leave you.
It's time to go, I suppose.
Thanks for visiting Spain with us.
Until next time, adios!

But there's something to remember
and please don't forget:
The more you learn of our world,
the smaller it can get.

The places can look different,
the people not like you,
but we all want the same in life:
Peace, Love, and Happiness—to name a few.

So when you go off traveling
to an amazing destination,
respect the people, culture, and land
and have an awesome vacation!

GLOSSARY:

Africa: a continent, see Map 1

architect: a person who creates plans to build buildings; one who studies architecture

architecture: the art and science of designing buildings

Catholic Monarchs: Ferdinand II of Aragon and Isabela I of Castile who brought together different parts of Spain after they were married. Spain grew under their rule, and as they gained more lands, they spread their religion of Catholicism (a kind of Christianity) and either drove out Muslims or converted them to Catholics.

Columbus: Christopher Columbus, an Italian explorer who was hired by Spain's King Ferdinand and Queen Isabella to sail westward to find Asia; the adventurer who is responsible for the European discovery of the Americas in 1492, using three ships: the Nina, the Pinta, and the Santa Maria
    *interesting fact: it was actually the ancient Greeks who figured out the earth is round about 2000 years ago; however, this fact was debated over the centuries until this fact was all but proven by this popular and well-known expedition of Columbus

conquests: invasions or land gains by use of military force

constitution: a set of rules that describes how a country works and the rights of the people that live there

Dali: Salvador Dali, a famous Spanish artist whose paintings look like strange dreams. His most famous painting is The Persistence of Memory which is a scene of a normal looking desert except that it has melted clocks, all telling different times. What do you think it all means?

destination: the place that you are going to

empire: people of a distant land who are ruled by an all-powerful king or queen; usually an empire uses force to rule people of different ethnic and cultural backgrounds

Europe: a continent, see Map 1

exotic: from another part of the world; often unusual, strange, and exciting

expand: to grow or make bigger

flamenco: a fast and lively kind of dance and music from the southern part of Spain

fusion: a way of bringing together two different things

Gaudi: Antoni Gaudi, a Spanish architect who created many of the buildings in Spain, especially Barcelona. He is famous for his special style. He worked on the Sagrada Familia church over half his life (he died at age 73, and worked on it for 43 years) and only a quarter of the project was done.

gothic: a style of architecture in Europe from the 12th–16th centuries; medieval-looking; also used to describe something dark, strange, and scary

invaded: entered into by force

matadors: bullfighters

merged: came together

migrants: people who go from one place to another, especially to find work or safety

Moors: the people from North Africa who invaded Spain. They practice the religion of Islam.

mosaics: artwork made by placing small pieces of stone, tile, or glass of different colors to make patterns or pictures

Muslim: a person or country who follows the religion of Islam. The most number of Muslim people live in the Middle East and North Africa; see Map 1

North Africa: the area in northern Africa, along the Mediterranean Sea; see Map 1

notorious: well known and famous, usually for something bad

Picasso: Pablo Picasso, a famous Spanish artist whose paintings described how he was feeling. When he was sad, he painted many sad and blue paintings (the Blue Period). When he fell in love, he painted loving, romantic, or happy paintings (the Rose Period). Then he tried other different kinds of styles that looked like something out of dreams or even nightmares (Cubism and Surrealism). Can you guess how he was feeling when he painted The Old Guitarist?

Romans: people from Rome, Italy; here, people from the Roman Empire-an empire that lasted for more than 400 years before splitting up. At one point, the Roman Empire owned land stretching across Europe, Africa, and Asia (mostly all the lands surrounding the Mediterranean Sea)

Spanish Inquisition: Spain's King Ferdinand and Queen Isabella used religion to control Spain and grow their kingdom by taking over foreign lands

surged: to suddenly and powerfully move up or increase

trade routes: a route or pathway used by ships over long distances in the ocean to buy and sell things

tread: to walk

Map 1.

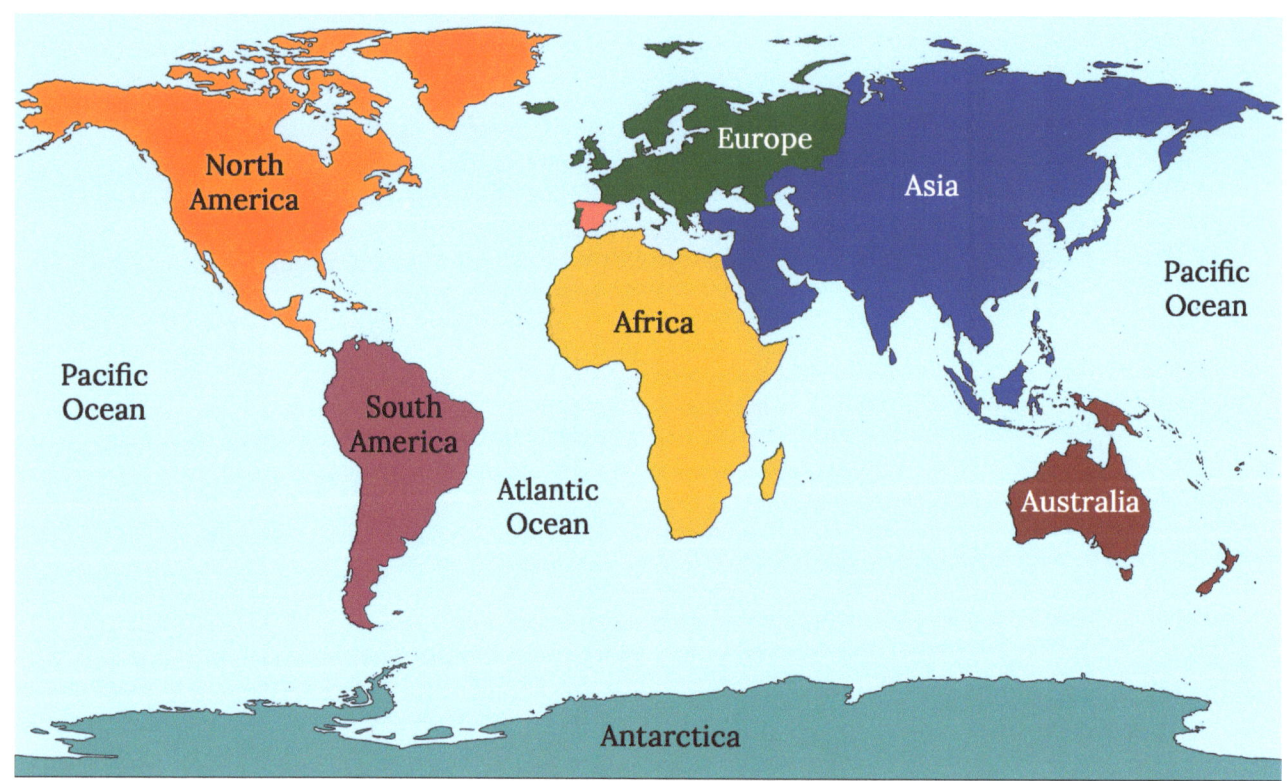

The continents of the world

Map 2.

Acknowledgements:

Thank you to Meredith Tennant. Your editorial skills have been most helpful!
Thank you to Lei Yang. You are the most efficient artist ever! Thank you so much for making this book come alive!
Thank you to my family for your patience during "busy mommy" times. Your encouragement and suggestions always bring a smile to my face. Nicholas and Adria, I love when you sit beside me making your own books. Those are really special moments. Salty, this book is dedicated to you, buddy. You are the salt of the earth and have been demoted not once but three times. You are the most patient of all. Nick, wo ai ni. I love you all omega times theta. --KN
p.s...As this book was being written in late 2017, Catalonia filed for secession from Spain.

© 2017 Salvador Dali, Fundacio Gala-Salvador Dali, Artists Rights Society

© 2017 Estate of Pablo Picasso / Artists Rights Society (ARS), New York

Copyright © 2017 by Kimberly Naylor
Illustrated by Lei Yang
Edited by Meredith Tennant
All rights reserved.

Travel Bug Press 2017
ISBN: 978-0-9979493-1-5